# IF I HAD THE FLOOR: warfare and doves' eyes

Star Bush

IF I HAD THE FLOOR: warfare and doves'
eyes © 2024 Star Bush




Presentation by *BookLeaf Publishing*

Web: www.bookleafpub.com

E-mail: info@bookleafpub.com


ISBN: 9789360942915

First edition 2024

# ACKNOWLEDGEMENT

I would like to thank my Lord and Savior, Jesus Christ, for every ounce of love that he has demonstrated towards me and has made its way into this book by acknowledging that the WORD of GOD is TRUTH and can save one's life.

I would love to acknowledge my Lord and Savior, Jesus Christ, as being my everything once and for all time. I will also acknowledge both of my parents for any life-giving encouragement, advice and humor given through them in order to help me or bring me to joy. Any other person who has ever motivated, prayed for or showed concern towards me over the course of my lifetime, I appreciate you much.

# PREFACE

These pieces reflect on light moments of hard times. This book is meant for the person who does not know the meaning of their struggles in life; to remind them that we all struggle and can overcome it through Christ. These pieces are meant to give hope, understanding and encouragement. Let it be known, also, that I do not bear false witness because I do not claim that every piece written in this book is directly related to my own struggles.

# HONORABLE MENTIONS

I wasn't looking into the mirror; I was only
visualizing my face.
I could see all its features and the shape of them
clearly, inside of my mind.
I was happy with it.
My demeanor made it hard for people to believe
what I was going through.
My dad and I had private conversations where I
cried, and he cheered me up.
He had made it through a lot, and I resemble
him.
I can remember how I thought to myself:
My strong mind has been inherited.

Coming home from the hospital felt better than
going there.
There was a separation between what I was and
what I was not going through.
Despite all warfare happening,
I knew that my mother did care about me
because of how she was acting.
Other people would not have understood this,
but I did.
She had been through a lot, and I resemble her.

As her sleepy eyes widened and her concerned
lips parted to calmly ask,
"Are you feeling ok today?"
I remember how I thought to myself:
My faith has been inherited.

# In the midst of a storm

Through GOD'S GRACE
I Won A Battle

I Rose Up
&
Threw Confetti

I stood UPRIGHT
&
continued regular life

I would
step
down

if it
meant
CHRIST

I   wear   a   crown   for   that

# Giving and Receiving

Powerful and promising communication with the creator.
Rivers flowing, prophetically.
Amens increasing, overtime.
Yielding fruit that is good.
Ending with Christ still on the mind.
Repenting, resting and repeating.

# Dancing on a grave problem

There was a small bug with six paper-thin legs minding its business on MY window-sill.

I killed it with the hard rubber-sole of one of my tap dancing shoes.

No remorse; Only gratification.

# A fight against the quarter of a time

While everyone else is self–healing
And other gentle things,
she longs to release war cries,
LOUDLY.

Please excuse her for the quarter of a time where
she may be:
Throwing tomatoes,
Hanging off of semi-trucks,
Going at least 80 MPH.

She would LOVE to walk RIGHT at all times.
But she could live in the quarter of a time for
seasons.

# Something Friendly
# Something Pure

I am trustworthy.
But I am rough.
You are too gentle for me
to trust myself with all of your deepness.

I have softness.
I would share that with you.
I have used it before to be soft with soft people.

I am capable of balance.
It is too LOUD for softer people.

# Abiding in HIM

8

GOD,


I am not sure if I have made mistakes that has
Tilted
This
World.



But,



I    had  my    COMPASS.



I
did not forget
THE WORD.



THANK GOD!

# THE LIGHT OF CHRIST

Being left to yourself,
could never mean
    being alone.
If, of course, you are
        TRUSTING
        IN THE LIGHT.

# 7 Pillars

Pleasing God more often.
Reading the Word daily.
Overcoming obstacles and hard times.
Verses being highlighted throughout.
Every day, pushing right back in.
Remembering scripture on purpose.
Building good character that pleases the Lord.
Strengthening the spirit through focusing on God.

# PUSHING love through

I love those who love me with their heart.
I love those who love me with their spirit.
I love those who love me with their mind.
I love those who love me with their flesh-
                With caution,

                I love.

I love those who love me with their soul.
I have loved those who have misused and
mishandled.

Love,
  I love God
      A lot.

                Some fight;
                Some don't.

Some fight to continue;
They fight to continue loving.

                    Fight to continue loving.

Love,
I know that fight.

Trust not in my heart or yours;
Just continue.

Now,
For Christ's sake,
FIGHT!

# HOPE in a forest

If I MUST survive
THEN


Trees are for SHADE
Leaves are to HEAL
Berries are to PICK
And EAT


HOWEVER


I want
NOTHING
to do
WITH A SPIDER'S WEB

# My Dear

Some people believe that
they are justified
to do some evil.
But you, My Dear,
You remember the truth!

Some people are jealous,
for whatever reason,
they alter pictures.
But you, My Dear,
you remember the truth!

In all your struggles,
in all your let downs.
With all your heart,
My Dear,
remember the truth!

# Hope in the LORD

Hosts of the Heavens!
There is a position for me.
I am trusting to please Christ,
by becoming as a tree.

# Punchline Truth

Most evil words,
by me, they go unheard.
But what really could not hurt me,
Is if someone threw out ALL the beef jerky.

# sweet aroma

17

Pushing resistance away and pulling faith in.
Remembering the Word and all of its richness.
Allowing God's presence to rise up.
Idols being torn down and removed.
Seeing everything much clearer.
Evil being destroyed by its root.

Defeating evil forces.
Allowing Christ to take over.
Needing to hear God's voice.
Casting away evil thoughts.
Increasing Hallelujahs.
No attention paid toward desolations.
Gaining wisdom, understanding and insight.

# BALANCE: THE LIGHT OF CHRIST BLOOMING IN DARK PLACES

If, of course,      it is      leaning on THE LIGHT,
                  then
All things are     capable     of BLOOMING IN  DARK PLACES.

# Belonging to Christ

LOVE did call him before.
And immediately,
he decided,
that there were things that he needed gone.


And so, he proceeded to fight
against all things that had never belonged there:
In the place of HONOR, where it did not belong.


In that path, things got tough.
After persistence, things got better.
LOVE did call him before; It was calling him to HONOR.

# Behind a shield at the front line

Love had me fighting.

I was mad!

Was I mad at God?